you don't have to be MAD to TRAVEL BY AIR

.......but it helps ! !

Published in the UK by
POWERFRESH Limited
Gray Street
Northampton
NN1 3QQ

Telephone 01604 30996
Facsimile 01604 21013

over and interior layout by Powerfresh

ou don't have to be mad to travel by air but it helps
BN 1 874125 538

nted in the UK by Avalon Print Northampton
Powerfresh August 1996

FISH 'N' CHIPS
CLOSED FOR ANNUAL HOLIDAY
WE'RE FLYING TONIGHT!

WHICH AIRPORT DO YOU FANCY SPENDING OUR HOLIDAY AT THIS YEAR?
SPAIN
THREAT OF STRIKE BY AIRLINE PILOTS

AND WHICH FILM WILL THEY BE SHOWING ON THE FLIGHT ?
TRAVEL AGENT
SPAIN
CRUISE

IT'S NOT FLYING THAT WORRIES ME – IT'S CRASHING THAT I'M SCARED OF!!

WE'RE TRAVELLING ON ONE OF THOSE JUMBO JETS!

I'D LIKE A SEAT NEXT TO THE EMERGENCY EXIT, PLEASE !!
FAREAIR
F 1071

IN AN EFFORT TO KEEP THE PLANE BALANCED, I'M AFRAID YOU'LL HAVE TO SIT ON OPPOSITE SIDES!

FLAIRAIR
PSST! ANY CHANCE OF PUTTING HIS GOLF CLUBS ON A DIFFERENT PLANE?

WHAT MAKES YOU THINK I'M NERVOUS ABOUT FLYING?
DEPARTURES

SORRY TO DISTURB YOU, SIR, BUT I THOUGHT YOU'D LIKE TO KNOW THAT YOUR FLIGHT HAS BEEN DELAYED A FURTHER TWELVE HOURS !!

I WISH I WAS TRAVELLING ON THAT PLANE !!

IT'S THE FIRST TIME HE'S EVER FLOWN!

EXCUSE ME, MADAM, BUT I THINK YOU'RE SITTING IN THE WRONG SEAT. MAY I SEE YOUR BOARDING PASS!

YOU CAN'T BE FEELING SICK — WE HAVEN'T LEFT THE GROUND YET!

SORRY ABOUT THE DELAY, LADIES AND GENTLEMEN, BUT THEY WON'T LET THE PILOT TAKE OFF UNTIL HE'S SOBERED UP!

WE WILL NOW DEMONSTRATE WHAT TO DO IN THE EVENT OF AN EMERGENCY!
HELP, WE'RE GOING TO CRASH!!
HELP!!

I WONDER WHICH PLANE OUR LUGGAGE IS ON?

£38 FOR A RETURN FLIGHT TO AMERICA ! I KNEW THERE HAD TO BE A CATCH !!
FAREAIR

I WISH YOU'D TRY AND RELAX A LITTLE, DEAR!

...ER, WOULD YOU MIND ASKING THE PILOT TO TURN BACK, PLEASE – MY HUSBAND'S NOT SURE WHETHER OR NOT HE LOCKED THE CAR!

AND **THAT** MUST BE THE 'IN FLIGHT' ENTERTAINMENT!

THIS AIRLINE OPERATES A STRICT NO SMOKING POLICY, SIR!

YOU SURELY DON'T BELIEVE ALL THAT NONSENSE ABOUT AIRCRAFT DISAPPEARING IN THE BERMUDA TRIANGLE, DO YOU?

SHE DIDN'T TAKE TOO KINDLY TO THAT CHAP PINCHING HER BOTTOM, DID SHE ?

LOOK WHAT I FOUND ON THE FLIGHT DECK, DAD!

OH, DEAR!
IT LOOKS AS IF OUR TOMMY'S BEEN ANNOYING THE PILOT AGAIN!!

HAVE YOU TRIED SUCKING ON A BOILED SWEET?
POP!
POP! POP!

OOER! THIS FLYING LARK'S A BIT SCAREY, ISN'T IT?

YOU'D BETTER TAKE AN EXTRA SICK BAG – YOU'LL PROBABLY NEED IT AFTER YOU'VE EATEN THAT!!

THAT MUST BE THE AUTOMATIC PILOT !!

FIRST THE GOOD NEWS! THERE'S JUST ENOUGH PARACHUTES FOR THE PILOT AND THE REST OF THE CABIN CREW....

I COULD BE WRONG, BUT I THINK WE'VE JUST LOST A WING !!

I WANT TO COMPLAIN ABOUT THE AMOUNT OF LEG ROOM ON THIS PLANE !!

THIS IS THE CAPTAIN SPEAKING.... LOOK, I'M NOT TOO SURE WHERE WE ARE AT THE MOMENT, SO IF YOU COULD ALL TAKE A LOOK OUT OF THE WINDOW AND LET ME KNOW IF YOU SEE A BIT OF LAND YOU RECOGNIZE, I'D BE MOST GRATEFUL!

HEY! ISN'T THAT THE PILOT?!!

THAT'S NOT A GOOD SIGN!!

HE SAYS SHE'S HIS SECRETARY!
BUSINESS CLASS

I CAN SEE HIS BALD SPOT, MUMMY!

LET'S PLAY A LITTLE GAME. LET'S TRY AND GUESS WHAT WE'RE EATING!

WELL WHAT DO YOU EXPECT FOR THE PRICE YOU'VE PAID!
BAKED BEANS
BAKED BEANS
BAKED BEANS
CHEAPO AIRLINES

EXCUSE ME, MISS... WHERE CAN I CHANGE INTO MY PYJAMAS ?

WE SEEM TO BE EXPERIENCING QUITE A BIT OF TURBULENCE!!

ISN'T THAT A WONDERFUL VIEW, DARLING?

IS THERE A DOCTOR ON BOARD, AND...ER, HAS ANYONE HERE EVER FLOWN A PLANE BEFORE?

I STILL RECKON WE'RE FLYING TOO LOW!!

NO! I DON'T WANT TO BECOME A MEMBER OF THE 'MILE HIGH' CLUB!!

THERE'S NO CAUSE FOR ALARM!

WHAT WERE YOU SAYING ABOUT FLYING BEING THE SAFEST FORM OF TRAVEL ?!!

WELL APART FROM THE MEAL DID YOU ENJOY THE FLIGHT ?

ZZZZZ
I THINK HE MUST HAVE TAKEN TOO MANY TRANQUILLIZERS!

CUSTOMS

GOODS TO DECLARE
NOTHING TO DECLARE
SHOULDN'T WE BE GOING THROUGH **THAT** ONE, DADDY?
DUTY FREE

HIC!
I'M AFRAID WE'LL HAVE TO CHARGE EXCESS DUTY ON YOU, SIR!
CUSTOMS
DUTY FREE

CAREFUL WITH YOUR TEDDY, DARLING — WE DON'T WANT TO BREAK THAT BOTTLE OF WHISKY INSIDE HIM, DO WE ?
CUSTOMS

THAT'S ANOTHER GOOD THING ABOUT BEING A PILOT — LOTS OF DUTY FREE!
WHISKY
VINO

CUSTOMS
LET'S CHECK HER LUGGAGE. I BET SHE'S GOT SOME SAUCY UNDERWEAR!!

CUSTOMS
CLINK!
CLINK!
CLINK!
DUTY FREE
CLINK!
CLINK!

HOW COME OUR CASE IS ALWAYS LAST?

ARRIVALS
MR. BROWN
JOAN BURTON
MR & MRS SIMPSON
JOHN CRABSON
ANY WOMAN WITH A 36·24·36 FIGURE!